KING SOLOMON'S GARDEN

POEMS AND ART INSPIRED BY THE OLD TESTAMENT

KING SOLOMON'S GARDEN

POEMS AND ART INSPIRED BY THE OLD TESTAMENT

SELECTED AND EDITED BY
LAURANCE WIEDER
HARRY N. ABRAMS, INC., PUBLISHERS

For my Mother,
and for my Father

frontispiece:
Rembrandt van Rijn. *Moses Breaking the Tablets of the Law.* 1659. Oil on canvas, 66⅜×53¼". Staatliche Museen zu Berlin, Preussischer Kulturbesitz Gemaldegalerie

title page:
Albert Bierstadt. *A Storm in the Rocky Mountains-Mt. Rosalie.* 1866. Oil on canvas, 83×142¼". The Brooklyn Museum, Brooklyn, New York. Dick S. Ramsay Fund, A. Augustus Healy Fund B, Frank L. Babbott Fund, A. Augustus Healy Fund, Ella C. Woodward Memorial Funds, Gift of Daniel M. Kelly, Gift of Charles Simon, Charles Smith Memorial Fund, Caroline Pratt Fund, Frederick Loeser Fund, Augustus Graham School of Design Fund, Bequest of Mrs. William T. Brewster, Gift of Mrs. W. Woodward Phelps, Gift of Seymour Barnard, Charles Stuart Smith Fund, Bequest of Laura L. Barnes, Gift of A. H. Bell, John B. Woodward Memorial Fund, Bequest of Mark Finley 76.79

endpapers:
Anonymous from Addis-Ababa. *Ethiopian Storyboard of the Queen of Sheba and King Solomon* (detail). n.d. 90½×34⅛". Collection Musée de l'Homme, Paris

Editor: ELLEN ROSEFSKY
Designer: DARILYN LOWE CARNES
Picture Research: NEIL RYDER HOOS

Library of Congress Cataloging-in-Publication Data

King Solomon's garden: poems and art inspired by the Old
 Testament / selected and edited by Laurance Wieder.
      p.   cm.
    ISBN 0–8109–3507–4
    1. Religious poetry, English.   2. Religious poetry,
American.   3. Bible. O.T.—History of Biblical events—
Poetry.   4. Bible—In art.   I. Wieder, Laurance, 1946–
PR1191.K48   1994
821.008′0382—dc20   93–47224

Copyright © 1994 Laurance Wieder

Published in 1994 by Harry N. Abrams, Incorporated,
New York
A Times Mirror Company

Printed and bound in Hong Kong

CONTENTS

PREFACE

"Thou that dwellest in the gardens, the companions hearken to thy voice: cause me to hear it."

—*Song of Songs 8:13*

I T IS TEMPTING to identify the garden of Solomon with the one in Eden, where Adam named all living things, and ate the fruit, and fell, taking language with him. But King Solomon, son of David the sweet singer of Israel and Bathsheba, built God's Temple in Jerusalem. Renowned for wisdom, he spoke "three thousand proverbs: and his songs were a thousand and five. And he spake of trees, from the cedar tree that is in Lebanon even unto the hyssop that springeth out of the wall: he spake also of beasts, and of fowl, and of creeping things, and of fishes." (*1Kings 4:29–33*) So Solomon's must be the walled garden of his *Song of Songs*, a setting for poetry.

This volume began as an anthology of poems inspired by passages in the Old Testament. The pictures were chosen later. Rather than illustrate the songs or Bible stories in one-for-one, slide-show fashion, I sought pictures that would comment upon, supplement, or otherwise illuminate the poems. The resulting assembly of word and image is best described as an old-fashioned, late twentieth-century emblem book, as an entertainment and as an aid to meditation.

The poems are arranged in roughly scriptural-chronological order, from *Genesis* through the *Book of Esther*. A few Psalm versions have been inserted during the life of David, in *1 and 2Samuel*. Poems inspired by the writings of the Prophets have been folded into the *Books of the Kings* and the *Chronicles*. The Songs and Wisdom books, ending out of order with *Ecclesiastes*, close the volume. Shuffled also by necessities of design and production, this plan still left room for variety, for delight in knowledge and the senses, the givens of art and poetry and the substance of religion.

For the most part, poems and images are reproduced entire. Where the poem is extracted from a longer work, the parent is identified. Some excerpted works such as "Paradise Lost," or Christopher Smart's "Song to David" may be familiar to readers, but "Egypt's Favorite," a 17th-century soap opera in verse, the "Triumph of Job," a verse paraphrase of the biblical book, and "Loves of David and Bethsabe," the only English Renaissance drama written on a biblical theme, are rarities. The captions indicate if a picture has been cropped or vignetted. The Bible itself offers pleasure and instruction piece by piece, sometimes letter by letter, each bit a part of the huge mosaic. And because these songs and pictures are scriptural, they are filled out, supported and informed by stories as old as they come, by laws commonly known and widely held, in language as strong and deep as it gets.

All the words and pictures in this book are "about" the real, what is known to be based on what the senses confirm, and what's been handed down over the generations. Whatever shape the poems take, however the images enter the seen, they are rooted in the out there, the not me. The persistence of that awe called the other distinguishes word of the living God from tales of fallen idols chanted in dead languages.

Where a painter can show how to see the old world in a new way, to witness scenes through another's eyes, the poet requires something else of the reader. Poetry makes a snapshot of a living voice, or perhaps a musical score for a speaker. To hear what is said as though it is another person talking, as directly and clearly as one's neighbor asking and answering, is the whole trick. To "make it new," as Ezra Pound instructed poets, is no mean feat when there is "no new thing under the sun." (The Talmud observes that there is a new moon every month, although the moon is not new.) Just what is true, and new, poses questions that turned Cavalier against Roundhead, set scribe against prophet, pits orthodoxy against reform—as though religion can be found in doctrine only, as though people are mere spirit without gravity.

There's a chance another Moses bearing Tablets of the Law might make our ruling straight, or that Elijah returned to earth by chariot could clarify soul and matter. Painters have imagined such scenes, and drawn them emblems. There is even a Psalm on the subject, the next-to-last:

New song? Nearly. Better
Hums through a kazoo than fancy fretwork
Strums to dazzle children.
Echoes in the shower, muffled bedroom
Cries: a two-edged sword:
It cuts the mute and those who should know better.
Writers without spirit
Cannot even praise the letter truly.

Laurance Wieder
Patchogue, New York

1

To the Public

from Jerusalem
William Blake

Reader! lover of books! lover of heaven,
And of that God from whom all books are given,
Who in mysterious Sinai's awful cave
To man the wondrous art of writing gave:
Again he speaks in thunder and in fire!
Thunder of Thought, and flames of fierce desire:
Even from the depths of Hell his voice I hear
Within the unfathomed caverns of my Ear.
Therefore I print; nor vain my types shall be:
Heaven, Earth and Hell henceforth shall live in harmony.

2.
LET THERE BE LIGHT!
D. H. Lawrence

If ever there was a beginning
there was no god in it
there was no Verb
no Voice
no Word.

There was nothing to say:
Let there be light!
All that story of Mr God switching on day
is just conceit.

Just man's conceit!
—Who made the sun?
—My child, I cannot tell a lie,
I made it!

George Washington's Grandpapa!

All we can honestly imagine in the beginning
is the incomprehensible plasm of life, of creation
struggling
and *becoming* light.

(see Genesis 1:3)

Lynd Ward. Plate from *Madman's Drum.*
1930. Wood engraving, 5½ × 3¾".
Copyright Estate of Lynd Ward

3.
GENESIS
Theodore Roethke

This elemental force
Was wrested from the sun;
A river's leaping source
Is locked in narrow bone.

This wisdom floods the mind,
Invades quiescent blood;
A seed that swells the rind
To burst the fruit of good.

A pearl within the brain,
Secretion of the sense;
Around a central grain
New meaning grows immense.

(see *Genesis 1:24*)

4.
THE ANIMALS
Edwin Muir

They do not live in the world,
Are not in time and space.
From birth to death hurled
No word do they have, not one
To plant a foot upon,
Were never in any place.

For with names the world was called
Out of the empty air,
With names was built and walled,
Line and circle and square,
Dust and emerald;
Snatched from deceiving death
By the articulate breath.

But these have never trod
Twice the familiar track,
Never never turned back
Into the memoried day.
All is new and near
In the unchanging Here
Of the fifth great day of God,
That shall remain the same,
Never shall pass away.

On the sixth day we came.

(see *Genesis 1:25*)

George Stubbs (1724–1806). *Lion and
Lioness.* Oil on canvas, 40½×50¼″.
Courtesy, Museum of Fine Arts, Boston.
M. Theresa B. Hopkins Fund

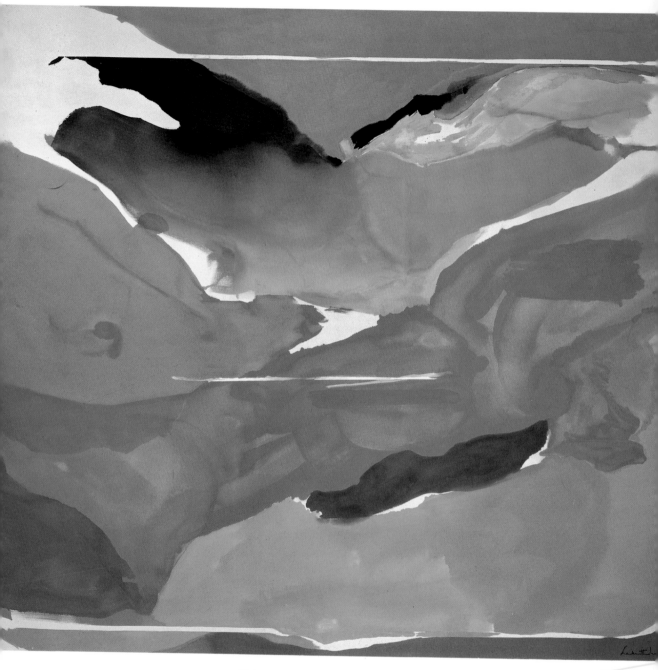

Helen Frankenthaler. *Nature Abhors a
Vacuum.* 1973. Acrylic on canvas,
8′7½″×9′4½″. Private collection

5

IN THE BEGINNING

Laura (Riding) Jackson

That was not the genesis:
This is the genesis.
That was the impregnation
Of the Mother by her children-to-be

Who in the fluster of forebeing
Cried out in voiceless voice:
"We are the Father!"
Then, voice of voice: "I am the Father's Son!"

To these it seemed long,
Counting from fathers to sons
To father still unborn.
Week on week they have said: "In seven days!"

The Mother has just begun to count
Her nine days of wonder.
She pauses upon the seventh—
Late on the seventh day is born her daughter.

In the first seven days of the Mother
Her sons are; they implore a Father,
They befoul their birth-places
And would be justified in this.

Late on the seventh day is born the daughter.
"Be you," the Mother says, "to them as father.
Absolve them of their flesh:
Do you wear flesh, and find goodness in it."

The last two days are to the daughter.
She is the Mother become sisterly
To be to the brother-sons as father.
"You have endured a week of you," she praises.

The seventh eve is therefore celebration.
Heavenly tomorrows lamp the night,
And every man's a universal favourite,
And none's a beggar because all are.

On the eighth day blind-spun spaces
Between man and man close in.
The universe of each and each has passed.
The daughter does not need to shout to be heard.

She opens the heads of her brothers
And lets out the aeroplanes.
"Now," she says, "you will be able to think better."
But their hearts still pump wildness into them.

Then a storm: love-ladies fly
Like empty leaves curled bodily.
From what trees fallen?
What infant gardens in the minds of men?

Then she encourages them to die
As many deaths they fear.
The physician-gods withdraw.
"Illness comes not to the dead."

Together all inspect the cups, the pencils,
The watches, matches, knives they have,
Some are from Tuesday's country, some from Friday's,
But nothing there from either Sunday.

Which so belabours their week's memories,
They sleep, and to the ninth day wake
In all-forgetful curiosity:
Amazed that they exist.

The daughter of the Mother tells a story.
They gape: can that have been?
Fair episodes they seem to recognize;
The evil part they execrate.

And so the ninth day sets,
Not seriate with an elder tenth
But usher to a younger first,
Unpentateuchal genesis.

(see *Genesis 2:1*)

6.

THE CREATION: A NEGRO SERMON

James Weldon Johnson

And God stepped out on space,
And He looked around and said:
I'm lonely—
I'll make me a world.

And as far as the eye of God could see
Darkness covered everything,
Blacker than a hundred midnights
Down in a cypress swamp.

Then God smiled,
And the light broke,
And the darkness rolled up on one side,
And the light stood shining on the other,
And God said: *That's good!*

Then God reached out and took the light in His hands,
And God rolled the light around in His hands
Until He made the sun;
And He set that sun a-blazing in the heavens.
And the light that was left from making the sun
God gathered it up in a shining ball
And flung it against the darkness,
Spangling the night with the moon and stars.

Then down between
The darkness and the light
He hurled the world;
And God said: *That's good!*

Romare Bearden. *Early Carolina
Morning.* 1979. Collage on board,
16×24″. Collection Dolores and Stanley
Feldman, Lynchburg, Virginia

Then God himself stepped down—
And the sun was on His right hand,
And the moon was on His left;
The stars were clustered about His head,
And the earth was under His feet.
And God walked, and where He trod
His footsteps hollowed the valleys out
And bulged the mountains up.

Then He stopped and looked and saw
That the earth was hot and barren.
So God stepped over to the edge of the world
And He spat out the seven seas—
He batted His eyes, and the lightnings flashed—
He clapped His hands, and the thunders rolled—
And the waters above the earth came down,
The cooling waters came down.

Then the green grass sprouted,
And the little red flowers blossomed,
The pine tree pointed his finger to the sky,
And the oak spread out his arms,
The lakes cuddled down in the hollows of the ground,
The rivers ran down to the sea;
And God smiled again,
And the rainbow appeared,
And curled itself around His shoulder.

Then God raised His arm and He waved His hand
Over the sea and over the land,
And He said: *Bring forth! Bring forth!*
And quicker than God could drop His hand,
Fishes and fowls
And beasts and birds
Swam the rivers and the seas,
Roamed the forests and the woods,
And split the air with their wings.
And God said: *That's good!*

Then God walked around,
And God looked around
On all that He had made.
He looked at His sun,
And He looked at His moon,
And He looked at His little stars;
He looked on His world
With all its living things,
And God said: *I'm lonely still.*

Then God sat down—
On the side of a hill where He could think;
By a deep, wide river He sat down;
With His head in His hands,
God thought and thought,
Till He thought: *I'll make me a man!*

Up from the bed of the river
God scooped the clay;
And by the bank of the river
He kneeled Him down;
And there the great God Almighty
Who lit the sun and fixed it in the sky,
Who flung the stars to the most far corner of the night,
Who rounded the earth in the middle of His hand;
This Great God,
Like a mammy bending over her baby,
Kneeled down in the dust
Toiling over a lump of clay
Till He shaped it in His own image;

Then into it He blew the breath of life,
And man became a living soul
Amen. Amen.

(see *Genesis 2:7*)

Claude Monet. *Monet's Garden at
Giverny.* 1900. Oil on canvas,
31⅞×36¼". Musée d'Orsay, Paris

7.
SONNET IV: THIS IS THE GARDEN
e. e. cummings

this is the garden: colors come and go,
frail azures fluttering from night's outer wing
strong silent greens serenely lingering,
absolute lights like baths of golden snow.
This is the garden: pursed lips do blow
upon cool flutes within wide glooms, and sing
(of harps celestial to the quivering string)
invisible faces hauntingly and slow.

This is the garden. Time shall surely reap
and on Death's blade lie many a flower curled,
in other lands where other songs be sung;
yet stand They here enraptured, as among
the slow deep trees perpetual of sleep
some silver-fingered fountain steals the world.

(see *Genesis 2:10*)

8.

ORIGINAL SEQUENCE
Philip Booth

Time was the apple Adam ate.
Eve bit, gave seconds to his mouth,
and then they had no minute left
to lose. Eyes opened in mid-kiss,
they saw, for once, raw nakedness,
and hid that sudden consequence
behind an hour's stripped leaves.

This is one sequence in the plot,
the garden where God came, that time,
to call. Hands behind him, walking
to and fro, he counted how
the fruit fell, bruised on frozen sod.
This was his orchard, his to pace;
the day was cool, and he was God.

Old Adam heard him humming, talking
to himself: *Winesap, King,*

> *ripen in sun,*
> *McIntosh and*
> *Northern Spy*
> *fall one by one,*
> *ripen to die.*

Adam heard him call his name,
but Adam, no old philosopher,
was not sure what he was after.
We're naked, Lord, and can't come out.
Eve nudged him with the bitter fruit.
God paused. *How do you know? Where is*
that woman that I sprung from you?

Eve held the twisted stem, the pulp;
she heard the low snake hiss, and let fly
blindly with a woman arm, careless
where her new-won anger struck.
The fodder for that two-fold flock
fell, an old brown core, at God's
stopped feet. He reached, and wound the clock.

(see Genesis 3:13)

René Magritte. *The Listening Room.*
1953. Oil on canvas, 31¼×39".
Whereabouts unknown

9.

INCARNATE DEVIL

Dylan Thomas

Incarnate devil in a talking snake,
The central plains of Asia in his garden,
In shaping-time the circle stung awake,
In shapes of sin forked out the bearded apple,
And God walked there who was a fiddling warden
And played down pardon from the heavens' hill.

When we were strangers to the guided seas,
A handmade moon half holy in a cloud,
The wisemen tell me that the garden gods
Twined good and evil on an eastern tree;
And when the moon rose windily it was
Black as the beast and paler than the cross.

We in our Eden knew the secret guardian
In sacred waters that no frost could harden,
And in the mighty mornings of the earth;
Hell in a horn of sulphur and the cloven myth,
All heaven in a midnight of the sun,
A serpent fiddled in the shaping-time.

(see *Genesis 3:6*)

Genesis page from *Moutier-Grandval Bible.* Illuminated manuscript. By permission of the British Library

Thomas Cole. *Expulsion from the Garden of Eden.* c. 1827–28. Oil on canvas, 39×54". Courtesy, Museum of Fine Arts, Boston. Gift of Mrs. Maxim Karolik for the Karolik Collection of American Paintings, 1815–1865

EDEN IS THAT OLD-FASHIONED HOUSE

Emily Dickinson

Eden is that old-fashioned House
We dwell in every day
Without suspecting our abode
Until we drive away.

How fair on looking back, the Day
We sauntered from the Door—
Unconscious our returning,
But discover it no more.

(see *Genesis 3:23*)

Ibn Bakhtishu. *Adam and Eve.* From
Manafi Al-Hayawan (Uses of Animals);
Maragha, M. 500, f. 4v). c. 1295.
Illuminated manuscript. The Pierpont
Morgan Library, New York

II.

TO THE GARDEN THE WORLD

Walt Whitman

To the garden the world anew ascending,
Potent mates, daughters, sons, preluding,
The love, the life of their bodies, meaning and being,
Curious here behold my resurrection after slumber,
The revolving cycles in their wide sweep having brought me again,
Amorous, mature, all beautiful to me, all wondrous,
My limbs and quivering fire that ever plays through them, for reasons, most
       wondrous,
Existing I peer and penetrate still,
Content with the present, content with the past,
By my side or back of me Eve following,
Or in front, and I following her just the same.

(see Genesis 3:23)

IMPERIAL ADAM

A. D. Hope

Imperial Adam, naked in the dew,
Felt his brown flanks and found the rib was gone.
Puzzled he turned and saw where, two and two,
The mighty spoor of Jahweh marked the lawn.

Then he remembered through mysterious sleep
The surgeon fingers probing at the bone,
The voice so far away, so rich and deep:
"It is not good for him to live alone."

Turning once more he found Man's counterpart
In tender parody breathing at his side.
He knew her at first sight, he knew by heart
Her allegory of sense unsatisfied.

The pawpaw drooped its golden breasts above
Less generous than the honey of her flesh;
The innocent sunlight showed the place of love;
The dew on its dark hairs winked crisp and fresh.

This plump gourd severed from his virile root,
She promised on the turf of Paradise
Delicious pulp of the forbidden fruit;
Sly as the snake she loosed her sinuous thighs,

And waking, smiled up at him from the grass;
Her breasts rose softly and he heard her sigh—
From all the beasts whose pleasant task it was
In Eden to increase and multiply

Michelangelo da Buonarroti. *The Creation of Man.* Portion of the Sistine Ceiling. Fresco, 1508–12. The Vatican, Rome

Adam had learned the jolly deed of kind:
He took her in his arms and there and then,
Like the clean beasts, embracing from behind,
Began in joy to found the breed of men.

Then from the spurt of seed within her broke
Her terrible and triumphant female cry,
Split upward by the sexual lightning stroke.
It was the beasts now who stood watching by:

The gravid elephant, the calving hind,
The breeding bitch, the she-ape big with young
Were the first gentle midwives of mankind;
The teeming lioness rasped her with her tongue;

The proud vicuña nuzzled her as she slept
Lax on the grass; and Adam watching too
Saw how her dumb breasts at their ripening wept,
The great pod of her belly swelled and grew,

And saw its water break, and saw, in fear,
Its quaking muscles in the act of birth,
Between her legs a pigmy face appear,
And the first murderer lay upon the earth.

(see Genesis 4:1)

Henri Rousseau. *The Merry Jesters.*
c. 1906. Oil on canvas, 57⅜×44⅝".
Philadelphia Museum of Art. The
Louise and Walter Arensberg Collection

ABEL'S BLOOD
Henry Vaughan

Sad, purple well! whose bubbling eye
Did first against a murderer cry;
Whose streams still vocal, still complain
      Of bloody Cain,
And now at evening are as red
As in the morning when first shed.
      If single thou
(Though single voices are but low)
Couldst such a shrill and long cry rear
As speaks still in thy maker's ear,
What thunders shall those men arraign
Who cannot count those they have slain,
Who bathe not in a shallow flood,
But in a deep, wide sea of blood?
A sea, whose loud waves cannot sleep,
But deep still calleth upon deep:
Whose urgent sound like unto that
Of many waters, beateth at
The everlasting doors above,
Where souls behind the altar move,
And with one strong, incessant cry
Inquire *How long?* of the most high.
      Almighty Judge!
At whose just laws no just men grudge;
Whose blessed, sweet commands do pour
Comforts and joys, and hopes each hour
On those that keep them; O accept
Of his vowed heart, whom thou hast kept
From bloody men! and grant, I may
That sworn memorial duly pay
To thy bright arm, which was my light
And leader through thick death and night!

Aye, may that flood,
That proudly spilt and despised blood,
Speechless and calm, as infants sleep!
Or if it watch, forgive and weep
For those that spilt it! May no cries
From the low earth to high heaven rise,
But what (like his, whose blood peace brings)
Shall (when they rise) speak better things
Than Abel's doth! may Abel be
Still single heard, while these agree
With his mild blood in voice and will,
Who prayed for those that did him kill!

(see Genesis 4:10)

Timothy H. O'Sullivan. *A Harvest of Death, Gettysburg, Pennsylvania.* July 1863. Photograph published in Alexander Gardner's *Photographic Sketchbook of War*

14.

The Woman and the Angel
Robert Service

An angel was tired of heaven, as he lounged in the golden street;
His halo was tilted side-ways, and his harp lay mute at his feet;
So the Master stooped in His pity, and gave him a pass to go,
For the space of a moon, to the earth-world, to mix with the men below.

He doffed his celestial garments, scarce waiting to lay them straight;
He bade good-bye to Peter, who stood by the golden gate;
The sexless singers of heaven chanted a fond farewell,
And the imps looked up as they pattered on the red-hot flags of hell.

Never was seen such an angel—eyes of heavenly blue,
Features that shamed Apollo, hair of a golden hue;
The women simply adored him; his lips were like Cupid's bow;
But he never ventured to use them—and so they voted him slow.

Till at last there came One Woman, a marvel of loveliness,
And she whispered to him: "Do you love me?" And he answered that woman,
        "Yes."
And she said: "Put your arms around me, and kiss me, and hold me-so—"
But fiercely he drew back, saying: "This thing is wrong, and I know."

Then sweetly she mocked his scruples, and softly she him beguiled:
"You, who are verily man among men, speak with the tongue of a child.
We have outlived the old standards; we have burst, like an over-tight thong,
The ancient, outworn, Puritanic traditions of Right and Wrong."

Then the Master feared for His angel, and called him again to His side,
For oh, the woman was wondrous, and oh, the angel was tried!
And deep in his hell sang the Devil, and this was the strain of his song:
"The ancient, outworn, Puritanic traditions of Right and Wrong."

(see Genesis 6:2)

Ambrogio or Evangelista
Preda. *An Angel in Red with
a Lute.* c. 1486–90. Oil on
panel, 46¾×24″. National
Gallery, London

CAPTAIN NOAH

F. R. Higgins

Old Noah, trailing plummets, found
Green harbours on the heights—
As from his deck he watched
The showers spill
Their gospels of the rainbow round
An arch of seven lights,
That bridged the tides of peace about
Each hill.

He dropped the sail and so his keel
Was floating in repose,
Until young grasses grew
About the ark—
Then out went every gangway and
Bright earth was one carouse,
Till hoof and claw grew heavy with
The dark.

'Twas then old Noah slept in wine,
Full naked on the hills;
But who'd blame that brave captain
For his jar,
While we sit making whiskey, where
Night on each dark pool spills
Beatitudes from every moon
And star.

(see *Genesis 9:21*)

Frederic Church. *Aurora Borealis.* 1865.
Oil on canvas, 56⅛×83½″. National
Museum of American Art, Smithsonian
Institution, Washington, D.C. Gift of
Eleanor Blodgett

Two Tongues in a Tower

John Wheelwright

Back in the iron tower he said, "When I left the tower
the ground shook under foot." "Did the ground-swell shake

Pieter Bruegel. *Tower of Babel.* 1563. Oil
on panel, 44⅞ × 61″. Rare Books &
Manuscripts Division, The New York
Public Library, Astor, Lenox and Tilden
Foundation. Kunsthistorisches Museum,
Vienna

any more," she wondered, "than my legs trembled under me?
What had we, then, to fear but nerves teased by a wind?"
"Was it a wind or the earthquake?" he asked; "Do not open the window.
Unroll the graph. Plot curves. Compare; predict;
record; I have given the numbers." But her eyes, which proved his numbers
filled with tears as she heard the wet of the night ask:
"Were there voices calling?" Yes, the voices of thin fear,
sigh for calm, soaring tall to the iron, grim tower:

"This spent of calm is not the calm we want.
Half our dread is lest the tower fall in flood
or fissure." "How *can* you continue your figures?" she asks. "Or *you*,
your tears?" he answers, and quietly placing the casement *against*
the wind, calls out his report: "It is not the flood; but more
drought and wind. Not yet the earthquake," he says clearly,
"but a wind!" and locks the window. She: "They hear the wind,
Statistician, give them statistics." And he? "They ask for bread."
He has lost the key to the larder. The lid of the bread box
is too thickset for tack hammers. He will go on charting predictions.

But the tongued wings' eleventh hour broadcast
they must answer. Too soon now, mutinous and stern
mariners'll come with skeleton key and sledges, abrupt
on this tower to open the larder or with key and oil or with hammers . . .
"To give longshoremen a handout of dry loaves
and salt fish?" he will ask. "Yes. Fish, large
as loaves; loaves, large as baskets," she will answer.
"Shall weepers be fed also?" he'll wonder, as she'll wonder:
"Shall I have, then, more sufficient company of love,"
as when he said (half aloud) to himself; *"Hear that storm."*

(see *Genesis 11:1–9*)

43

17.

SARAH

Delmore Schwartz

The angel said to me: "Why are you laughing?"
"Laughing! Not me! Who was laughing? I did not laugh. It was
A cough. I was coughing. Only hyenas laugh.
It was the cold I caught nine minutes after
Abraham married me: when I saw
How I was slender and beautiful, more and more
Slender and beautiful.
                            I was also
Clearing my throat; something inside of me
Is continually telling me something
I do not wish to hear: A joke: A big joke:
But the joke is always just on me.
He said: you will have more children than the sky's stars
And the seashore's sands, if you just wait patiently.
Wait: patiently: ninety years? You see
The joke's on me!"

18.

ANOTHER SARAH

Anne Porter

for Christopher Smart

When winter was half over
God sent three angels to the apple-tree
Who said to her
"Be glad, you little rack
Of empty sticks,
Because you have been chosen.

In May you will become
A wave of living sweetness
A nation of white petals
A dynasty of apples."

(see Genesis 18:10–15)

44

Fairfield Porter. *Anne in Doorway.* 1974.
Oil on canvas, 47×37″. Collection of the
Heckscher Museum, Huntington, New
York. Gift of Mrs. Fairfield Porter

Artist unknown. *Lot and His Two Daughters with Lot's Wife as a Pillar of Salt.* Illustration from a 15th-century German bible

19.
Lot's Wife
Albert Goldbarth

You wouldn't recognize her, now.
And why should it be different for her?
The lineaments of being a person give way
to being an element of people.

Often we misuse her as a metaphor.
Legend means just that distance.
But real cattle, real sheep, licked cups
into her body.

Every night their tongues would do what
Gomorrah burned for. Animals don't know,
though, so are blameless. Then the rain, even
closer to God than an animal, licked her completely gone.

She only wanted to see the sky split open.
Surely everybody has wanted to see the sky split open?
She is here when we pour at our table.
She is here when we pour in our sleep.

(see *Genesis 19:26*)

Marc Chagall. *Eliezer and Rebecca*. 1931.
Oil and gouache, 26⅛×20½″. Musée
National du Marc Chagall (Message
Biblique), Nice

20.

GENESIS XXIV

Arthur Hugh Clough

Who is this Man
    that walketh in the field,
O Eleazar,
    steward to my lord?

And Eleazar
    answered her and said,
Daughter of Bethuel,
    it is other none
But my lord Isaac,
    son unto my lord;
Who, as his wont is,
    walketh in the field
In the hour of evening
    meditating there.

Therefore Rebekah
    hasted where she sat,
And from her camel
    lighting to the earth
Sought for a veil,
    and put it on her face.

Wherefore he came,
    and met them on the field
Whom, when Rebekah
    saw, she came before,
Saying, Behold
    the handmaid of my lord,
Who for my lord's sake
    travel from my land.

But he said, O
    thou blessed of our God,
Come, for the tent
    is eager for thy face.
Shall not thy husband
    be unto thee more than
Hundreds of kinsmen
    living in thy land?

And Eleazar answered,
    Thus and thus,
Even according
    as thy father bade,
Did we; and thus and
    thus it came to pass;
Lo! is not this
    Rebekah, Bethuel's child?

And as he ended
    Isaac spoke and said,
Surely my heart
    went with you on the way,
When with the beasts
    ye came unto the place.

Truly, O child
    of Nahor, I was there,
When to thy mother
    and thy mother's son
Thou madest answer,
    saying, I will go.
And Isaac brought her
    to his mother's tent.

(see Genesis 24:65)

THE JACOB'S LADDER

Denise Levertov

The stairway is not
a thing of gleaming strands
a radiant evanescence
for angels' feet that only glance in their tread, and need not
touch the stone.

It is of stone.
A rosy stone that takes
a glowing tone of softness
only because behind it the sky is a doubtful, a doubting
night gray.

A stairway of sharp
angles, solidly built.
One sees that the angels must spring
down from one step to the next, giving a little
lift of the wings:

and a man climbing
must scrape his knees, and bring
the grip of his hands into play. The cut stone
consoles his groping feet. Wings brush past him.
The poem ascends.

(see *Genesis 28:12*)

Copy after Domenico Fetti. *Jacob's
Dream.* c. 1589–1624. Oil on canvas,
32×24″. The Cleveland Museum of Art,
Gift of Myron H. Wilson, 40.437

Si uiure la
me qui sicr de
scure zse pla
inra son seig
nce de ioseph
z dist qe celi a il
ser. z le nostre
au doit.

Or z uienr
Butifar z le
ser prendre
z li er. z ba
tre

A ame qui
clama a son
seignor z se
plainst de ioseph se
nesie la synago
ge qui se clama al
phylosofes z se
plainst de ihucrist.
z le nostre au doit

Butifar qi con
manda qe ioseph fust
pris z ferz z batuz
senefie Pilate qi co
manda a si gienf qe
ihucrist fust pris
z batuz z crucefiez

li uiena li
serienz But
far z mist io
seph en la char
tre z li pison
qen la charte fu
runr la ceinr z li
tendirent les
mains

Li e ioseph en
la charte z li
pancier z un
boreillers auec
lui. li boreillers
a destre z li pan
ciers a senestre.

Et qe ioseph
fu mis en la char
tre z li prisonier
la ceinr z ten
dirent les mains
senefie qe ihucrist de
scend en la charte
d enfer z li pome
z les bones ppphes
li rendent lor ma
ins z la ceinr

I osef qi fu en
la charte sene
fie ihucrist qi
fu el mund li
boreillers qi erra de
stre senefie cels qi un
urenr bone oeure
a destre li panciers
qi fu a senestre sene
fie cels qi daimeur
en mauueses oeure
a senestre

22.

Joseph's Coat

George Herbert

> Wounded I sing, tormented I indite,
> Thrown down I fall into a bed, and rest:
> Sorrow hath changed its note: such is his will,
> Who changeth all things, as him pleaseth best.
> For well he knows, if but one grief and smart
> Among my many had his full career,
> Sure it would carry with it even my heart,
> And both would run until they found a bier
> To fetch the body; both being due to grief.
> But he hath spoiled the race; and given to anguish
> One of joy's coats, ticing it with relief
> To linger in me, and together languish.
> I live to show his power, who once did bring
> My joys to weep, and now my griefs to sing.

(see *Genesis 37*)

23

Joseph in Carcere: or, The Innocent Prisoner

from *Egypt's Favorite*

Francis Hubert

Me thinks I see him looking on his hands
Fast bound with chains, which unto heaven he rears;
And are (says he) these heavy iron bands
The golden bracelets that poor virtue wears?

Had my too cruel brothers been so chained
I had not then been thus in prison pent.
Such manacles their furies had restrained
And I had been as free, as innocent.

Or had I with my Lady changed embraces
When in her arms she would have clasped me fast,
I had not tasted then of these disgraces,
Which will (I fear) prove fatal at the last.

Virtue, I thought, had been a real thing,
But now I find that 'tis an airy name:
Hate did my brothers, lust my Lady sting,
Yet neither they nor she feel smart or blame.

But I that only a mere patient was
And not an agent with them in their sin;
'Tis I alone that undergo the lash
And I must smart for what they faulted in.

Me thinks my crop should have been like my seed—
I planted virtue, that sweet smelling rose,
And can that root such stinging nettles breed?
But there is use of nettles, so of foes.

Why was I called "Joseph"? that's "Increasing,"
And do not I increase in misery?
My name was rightly given, for without ceasing
My strange disasters daily multiply.

Yet Job had been a fitter name for me:
"Job," "Sorrowful," or "Hated," which you will:
For that sad name doth both ways well agree
With those sad fortunes that pursue me still.

For am I not a man made up of sorrow,
Whose matter and whose form is wretchedness?
Unhappy now, but shall be more tomorrow,
My days are but additions to distress.

That sun that sees me breathing out my ill
Will shortly see me without any breath:
Malice and means, a woman and her will,
Lust and neglect; the very sounds of death.

And that will be the period of my pain,
The short and sweet compendium of all woe:
Weak-hearted Joseph, raise thy spirits again,
Collect thy self, be not dejected so!

Oft hast thou heard thy father Jacob say
There was a Libra 'mongst the signs of heaven
Who always did in equal balance weigh
The acts of men and kept the scales most even.

And without doubt when thou art truly weighed
Thou shalt go current, though thou suffer now:
Heaven must not be contested but obeyed,
To whose just ends all mortals needs must bow.

And, Joseph, he that raised thee from the pit
When thy enraged brothers played their part
Can find both time and means, when he thinks fit,
To free thee from this dungeon where thou art.

But say he do not, why should wretched dust
Be so much daring as to question God?
Whose councils oft are secret, ever just:
If therefore still he please to use the rod,

Be it for me, I have for my defence
Armor of proof to bear all blows withal,
A spotless and a peaceful conscience,
And that is safer then a brazen wall.

And, Joseph, though thy sufferings be most great
Yet think upon the letters of thy name,
Which being inverted bring some comfort yet:
For (Hope Is) is Ioseph his anagram:

And there is hope; nay, there's assurance rather
Where God is pleased to interpose his hand,
Who, out of poisons, antidotes doth gather,
As by the story here we understand:

For in close prison where poor Joseph lies
Mewed up in bolts and chains to death and shame,
Pursued by many dangerous enemies,
The abused agents of a lustful Dame;

There (even unlooked-for there) upon a day
(And sure 'twas God that put it in his mind)
The jailer thought his prison to survey,
Where many souls and foul ones he doth find.

(see *Genesis 39–40*)

Giovanni Battista Piranesi. *Prison.*
c. 1760. Etching, 15⅜×9½″. Collection
Museo de Bellas Artes, Caracas,
Venezuela

Sir Lawrence Alma-Tadema. *The Finding
of Moses.* 1904. Oil on canvas, 54⅛×
84″. Private collection

24.

MOSES IN INFANCY
Jones Very

How! Canst thou see the basket wherein lay
The infant Moses by the river's side,
And her who stood and watched it on the tide;
Will time bring back to thee that early day?
And canst thou to the distant Nile be near,
Where lived that mother, tossed with hope and fear
Yet more than was her infant by the wave?
No: Time will not his dark domain unbar;
Himself he cannot from oblivion save,
Nor canst thou make come nearer what is far;
But thou hast human sympathies to feel
What eye, nor ear, nor sense can e'er reveal;
Hope too is thine, that past the ocean sails,
And memory, that over time himself prevails!

(see *Exodus 2:3*)

J. M. W. Turner. *The Fifth Plague of Egypt.* 1800. Oil on canvas, 48×72″. Indianapolis Museum of Art; Anonymous Gift in memory of Evan F. Lilly

25.

EXODUS

George Oppen

Miracle of the children   the brilliant
Children   the word
Liquid as woodlands   Children?

When she was a child I read Exodus
To my daughter   "The children of Israel . . ."

Pillar of fire
Pillar of cloud

We stared at the end
Into each other's eyes   Where
She said hushed

Were the adults   We dreamed to each other
Miracle of the children
The brilliant children   Miracle

Of their brilliance   Miracle
of

(see *Exodus 14:29*)

60

26.

TABERNACLE

D. H. Lawrence

Come, let us build a temple to oblivion
with seven veils, and an innermost
Holy of Holies of sheer oblivion.

And there oblivion dwells, and the silent soul
may sink into god at last, having passed the veils.

But anyone who shall ascribe attributes to God or oblivion
let him be cast out, for blasphemy.
For God is a deeper forgetting far than sleep
and all description is a blasphemy.

(see Exodus 40)

Ben Shahn. *Identity.* 1968. Mixed media,
40×27½". Thyssen-Bornemisza
Collection, Lugano, Switzerland

27.

Day of Atonement

Charles Reznikoff

The great Giver has ended His disposing;
the long day
is over and the gates are closing.
How badly all that has been read
was read by us,
how poorly all that should be said.

All wickedness shall go in smoke.
It must, it must!
The just shall see and be glad.
The sentence is sweet and sustaining;
for we, I suppose, are the just;
and we, the remaining.

If only I could write with four pens between five fingers
and with each pen a different sentence at the same time—
but the rabbis say it is a lost art, a lost art.
I well believe it. And at that of the first twenty sins that we confess,
five are by speech alone;
little wonder that I must ask the Lord to bless
the words of my mouth and the meditations of my heart.

Now, as from the dead, I revisit the earth and delight
in the sky, and hear again
the noise of the city and see
earth's marvelous creatures—men.
Out of nothing I became a being,
and from a being I shall be
nothing—but until then
I rejoice, a mote in Your world,
a spark in Your seeing.

(see *Leviticus 16*)

28.

A Paraphrase on Leviticus Chapter XI, After the Manner of Master Geoffrey Chaucer in His Assembly of Fowls

Thomas Warton the Elder

Of feathered fowls, that fan the buxom air,
Not all alike were made for food to men;
For, these thou shalt not eat, doth God declare,
Twice ten their number, and their flesh unclean:
First the great eagle, bird of feigned Jove,
Which Thebans worship, and diviners love:

Next ossifrage, and osprey, (both one kind)
Of luxury, and rapine, emblems meet,
That haunt the shores, the choicest prey to find,
And burst the bones, and scoop the marrow sweet:
The vulture, void of delicace, and fear,
Who spareth not the pale dead man to tear:

The tall-built swan, fair type of pride confessed;
The pelican, whose sons are nursed with blood,
Forbid to man!—She stabbeth deep her breast,
Self-murderess through fondness to her brood:
They too that range the thirsty wilds among,
The ostriches, unthoughtful of their young:

The raven ominous, (as Gentiles hold)
What time she croaketh hoarsely *A la Morte*;
The hawk, aerial hunter, swift, and bold,
In feats of mischief trained for disport;
The vocal cuckoo, of the falcon race,
Obscene intruder in her neighbor's place:

Fritz Eichenberg. *Nightwatch*. 1962.
Wood engraving, 13×13″. The Estate of
Fritz Eichenberg

The owl demure, who loveth not the light,
(Ill semblance she of wisdom to the Greek)
The smallest fowls' dread foe, the coward kite,
And the still heron, arresting fishes meek;
The glutton cormorant, of sullen mood:
Regarding no distinction in her food.

The stork, which dwelleth on the fir treetop,
And trusteth that no power shall her dismay,
As kings on their high stations place their hope,
Nor wist that there be higher far than they:
The gay ger-eagle, beautiful to view,
Bearing within a savage heart untrue:

The ibis whom in Egypt Israel found,
Fell bird! That living serpents can digest;
The crested lapwing, wailing shrill around,
Solicitous, with no contentment blessed:
Last the foul bat, of bird, and beast first bred,
Flitting, with little leathern sails dispread.

(see *Leviticus 11:13–19*)

29

ON BALAAM, AND HIS ASS

Henry Colman

Whither, thou son of Beor, hastes thou so,
Or why with these associates dost thou go?
   Doth it befit
A man of God with such as these to sit?
   Art thou become
A Moabite with them? or hath the sum
Of divination brought thee made thee fear
   No fate, nor care
  For thy great Lord's commands?
O powerful wealth, when such an one as this
Will leave his God for gold, forsake his land
And go with strangers, forfeit his soul's bliss.

Thinkst thou, thou canst with safety reach the end
Of thy forbidden journey, and attend
   On Moab's king
Though God forbid thee? know that God will bring
   Unlooked-for ill
Upon thy head, horror and grief shall fill
Thy understanding part, thy fainting ass
   Would bid thee pass
  No further, could she speak;
But thou wilt on though a sword's point's in the way
To stop thy passage, and resolved wilt break
Through, although an angel bid thee stay.

The seer is become a verier ass
Than is the beast he rides on, and alas
   But for that beast,
Had ere he further passed, been left to feast
   The impartial worms:
And while he kicks, and beats, and fumes, and storms

Francisco Goya. *Tu que no puedes (They Cannot Help It)*. Plate 42 from *Los Capricios*. 1799. Etching and burnished aquatint, 8½×5⅞″. Courtesy of The Hispanic Society of America, New York

'Gainst the poor ass, the ass bespeaks him thus:
Is this righteous,
Thrice to correct me, when
I am not faulty? am not I your ass
Which all your life you've rid on? wherefore then
(Since never used to fail, forbid to pass

By the angel's threatening hand who thwarts your way)
Spend you your rage on me? be wise, and stay.
Nor could this strange,
Unheard-of miracle in the beast once change
His firm intent,
But she should die had he a sword, so bent
He was on his own will that on he would.
Oh, that man should
Be so rebellious still
Against his God's commands; himself had put
His reason's eyes out, and depraved his will,
And God in justice did his body's shut:

But now he sees the angel, and in show
Would have returned, but is commanded go
His journey on.
Glad of command he goes, although
Because it was
Indeed his own desire, so that (alas)
The precept proves his curse, himself shall loose
Himself, nor choose
But bless, where he would curse;
And 'cause he would not virtuous live, shall die
Among the heathens like a beast, or worse.
Such is the end of base cupidity;

Contempt of's God, and fond desire of gain
Hath switched, and spurred him to eternal pain.

(see Numbers 22:22–35)

69

30

THE BOOK OF THE WORLD
William Drummond of Hawthornden

Of this fair volume which we "world" do name,
If we the sheets and leaves could turn with care,
Of Him who it corrects, and did it frame,
We clear might read the art and wisdom rare?
Find out his power which wildest powers doth tame,
His providence extending everywhere,
His justice which proud rebels doth not spare.
In every page, no, period of the same:
But silly we (like foolish children) rest
Well pleased with colored vellum, leaves of gold,
Fair dangling ribbons, leaving what is best,
On the great Writer's sense ne'er taking hold;
   Or if by chance our minds do muse on aught,
   It is some picture on the margin wrought.

(see *Deuteronomy* 31:24–26)

Master Hugo. Frontispiece of the Book
of Deuteronomy from the *Bury Bible.*
(Ms. 2, f. 94r.) 12th century.
Illuminated manuscript. Courtesy of the
Master and Fellows of Corpus Christi
College, Cambridge, England

Giovanni Segantini. *Rahab and the Messengers*. Galerie der Bildenden Kunst, Litomerice, Czechoslovakia

31.

WOMEN OF JERICHO
Phyllis McGinley

Though seven times, or seventy times seven,
Your armies circle our beleaguered town,
Not with their clamor may our gates be riven;
O, not by trumpets shall the walls go down!
Send out your troops to trample the fresh grasses
With horns and banners! They shall find defeat.
These walls can bear the insolence of brasses
Sounded at noonday in the dust and heat.

It is the whisper, only, that we dread:
The hushed and delicate murmur like low weeping
Which shall assail us, when, as do the dead,
The warders sleep and all the town lies sleeping.
That holy word is whispered which can fell
These armored walls, and raze the citadel.

(see *Joshua* 6)

32.

BLIND AMONG ENEMIES

from *Samson Agonistes*

John Milton

Blind among enemies, O worse than chains,
Dungeon, or beggary, or decrepit age!
Light the prime work of God to me is extinct,
And all her various objects of delight
Annulled, which might in part my grief have eased,
Inferior to the vilest now become
Of man or worm; the vilest here excel me,
They creep, yet see, I dark in light exposed
To daily fraud, contempt, abuse, and wrong,
Within doors, or without, still as a fool,
In power of others, never in my own;
Scarce half I seem to live, dead more than half.
O dark, dark, dark, amid the blaze of noon,
Irrecoverably dark, total eclipse
Without all hope of day!
O first created Beam, and thou great Word,
"Let there be light, and light was over all";
Why am I thus bereaved thy prime decree?
The sun to me is dark
And silent as the moon,
When she deserts the night
Hid in her vacant interlunar cave.
Since light so necessary is to life,
And almost life itself, if it be true
That light is in the soul,
She all in every part; why was the sight
To such a tender ball as the eye confined?
So obvious and so easy to be quenched,
And not as feeling through all parts diffused,
That she might look at will through every pore?
Then had I not been thus exiled from light;

As in the land of darkness yet in light,
To live a life half dead, a living death,
And buried; but O yet more miserable!
My self, my sepulcher, a moving grave,
Buried, yet not exempt
By privilege of death and burial
From worst of other evils, pains and wrongs,
But made hereby obnoxious more
To all the miseries of life,
Life in captivity
Among inhuman foes.

Adriaen van der Werff. (1659–1722). *Samson and Delilah.* National Gallery, Prague

(see *Judges 13–16*)

33

David's Song to Saul

from "A Song to David"
Christopher Smart

He sung of God—the mighty source
Of all things—the stupendous force
      On which all strength depends;
From whose right arm, beneath whose eyes,
All period, power, and enterprise
      Commences, reigns, and ends.

Angels—their ministry and meed,
Which to and fro with blessings speed,
      Or with their citterns wait;
Where Michael with his millions bows,
Where dwells the seraph and his spouse,
      The cherub and her mate.

Of man—the semblance and effect
Of God and Love—the Saint elect
      For infinite applause—
To rule the land, and briny broad,
To be laborious in his laud,
      And heroes in his cause.

The world—the clustering spheres he made,
The glorious light, the soothing shade,
      Dale, champaign, grove, and hill;
The multitudinous abyss,
Where secrecy remains in bliss,
      And wisdom hides her skill.

Trees, plants, and flowers—of virtuous root;
Gem yielding blossom, yielding fruit,
　　　Choice gums and precious balm;
Bless ye the nosegay in the vale,
And with the sweetness of the gale
　　　Enrich the thankful psalm.

Of fowl—e'en every beak and wing
Which cheer the winter, hail the spring,
　　　That live in peace or prey;
They that make music, or that mock,
The quail, the brave domestic cock,
　　　The raven, swan, and jay.

Of fishes—every size and shape,
Which nature frames of light escape,
　　　Devouring man to shun:
The shells are in the wealthy deep,
The shoals upon the surface leap,
　　　And love the glancing sun.

Of beasts—the beaver plods his task;
While the sleek tigers roll and bask,
　　　Nor yet the shades arouse;
Her cave the mining coney scoops;
Where o'er the mead the mountain stoops,
　　　The kids exult and browse.

Of gems—their virtue and their price,
Which hid in earth from man's device,
　　　Their darts of lustre sheathe;
The jasper of the master's stamp,
The topaz blazing like a lamp
　　　Among the mines beneath.

Blessed was the tenderness he felt
When to his graceful harp he knelt,
      And did for audience call;
When Satan with his hand he quelled,
And in serene suspense he held
      The frantic throes of Saul.

His furious foes no more maligned
As he such melody divined,
      And sense and soul detained;
Now striking strong, now soothing soft,
He sent the godly sounds aloft,
      Or in delight refrained.

(see 1Samuel 16:14–23)

Lucas van Leyden. *David Playing Before Saul*. c. 1508. Engraving, 10×7¼″. The Metropolitan Museum of Art, New York, Rogers Fund, 1918

34

I Took My Power in My Hand

Emily Dickinson

I took my Power in my Hand—
And went against the World—
'Twas not so much as David—had—
But I—was twice as bold—

I aimed my Pebble—but Myself
Was all the one that fell—
Was it Goliath—was too large—
Or was myself—too small?

(see *1 Samuel 17:32-51*)

Andrea del Castagno. *The Youthful
David.* c. 1450. Oil on leather mounted
on wood, height: 45½; width: 30¼ to
16⅛″. National Gallery of Art,
Washington, D.C. Widener Collection

35.

SAUL

George Noel Gordon, Lord Byron

> Thou whose spell can raise the dead,
>> Bid the prophet's form appear.
>> "Samuel, raise thy buried head!
>> King, behold the phantom seer!"
> Earth yawned; he stood the centre of a cloud:
> Light changed its hue, retiring from his shroud.
> Death stood all glassy in his fixed eye;
> His hand was withered, and his veins were dry;
> His foot, in bony whiteness, glittered there,
> Shrunken and sinewless, and ghastly bare;
> From lips that moved not and unbreathing frame,
> Like caverned winds, the hollow accents came.
> Saul saw, and fell to earth, as falls the oak,
> At once, and blasted by the thunderstroke.

>> "Why is my sleep disquieted?
>> Who is he that calls the dead?
>> Is it thou, O King? Behold,
>> Bloodless are these limbs, and cold:
>> Such are mine; and such shall be
>> Thine to-morrow, when with me:
>> Ere the coming day is done,
>> Such shalt thou be, such thy son.
>> Fare thee well, but for a day,
>> Then we mix our mouldering clay.
>> Thou, thy race, lie pale and low,
>> Pierced by shafts of many a bow;
>> And the falchion by thy side
>> To thy heart thy hand shall guide:
>> Crownless, breathless, headless fall,
>> Son and sire, the house of Saul!"

Salvator Rosa. *Saul and the Witch of Endor.* 107½×76″. Musée du Louvre, Paris

(see 1 Samuel 28)

36.

KING DAVID DANCES

John Berryman

Aware to the dry throat of the wide hell in the world,
O trampling empires, and mine one of them,
and mine one gross desire against His sight,
slaughter devising there,
some good behind, ambiguous ahead,
revolted sons, a pierced son, bound to hear,
mid hypocrites amongst idolaters,
mocked in abysm by one shallow wife,
with the ponder both of priesthood & of State
heavy upon me, yea,
all the black same I dance my blue head off!

(see *2Samuel 6*)

Chaim Gross. *Sketch of Dancing Hasidim.*
1959. Pencil, watercolor, and ink,
9⅞×30½″. Collection the Estate of
Chaim Gross

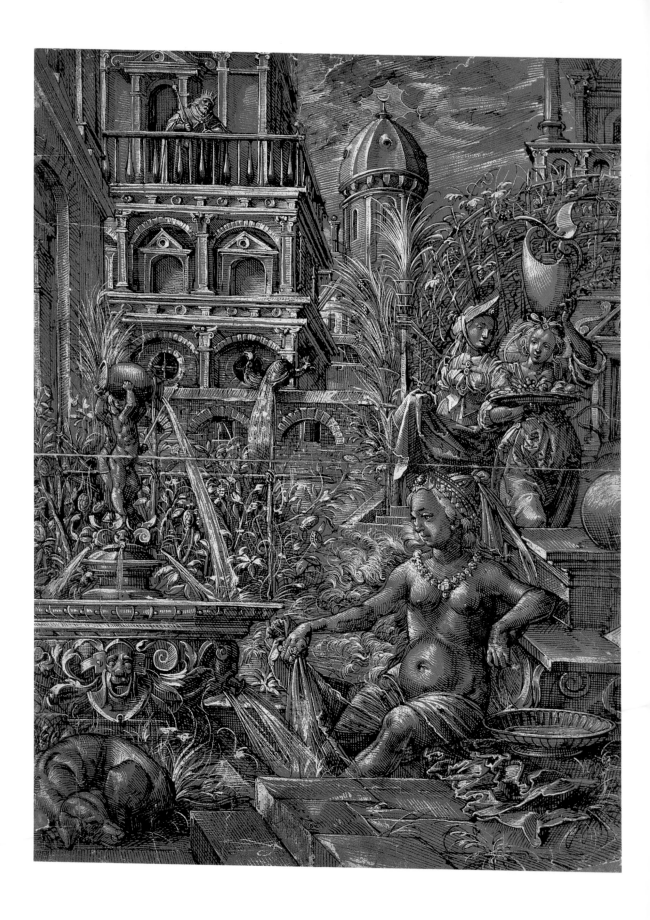

37.

SONG

from *The Love of King David and Fair Bethsabe*
George Peele

Hot sun, cool fire, tempered with sweet air,
Black shade, fair nurse, shadow my white hair.
Shine, sun; burn, fire; breathe, air, and ease me;
Shadow, my sweet nurse, keep me from burning,
Make not my glad cause cause of mourning.

    Let not my beauty's fire
    Inflame unstaid desire,
    Nor pierce any bright eye
    That wandereth lightly.

(see *2Samuel 11:2*)

Daniel Lindtmayer. *King David and Bathsheba.* 1578. Colored crayon, 15¼×11⅜". Oeffentliche Kunstsammlung Basel, Kupferstichkabinett

38

O Lord, Thou Hast Searched and Known Me

Mary Herbert, Countess of Pembroke

O Lord in me there lieth nought
    But to thy search revealed lies:
        For when I sit
        Thou markest it;
    No less thou notest when I rise.
Yea, closest closet of my thought
    Hath open windows to thine eyes.

Thou walkest with me when I walk;
    When to my bed for rest I go,
        I find thee there,
        And everywhere;
    Not youngest thought in me doth grow,
No, not one word I cast to talk,
    But yet unuttered thou dost know.

If forth I march, thou goest before,
    If back I turn, thou comst behind;
        So forth nor back
        Thy guard I lack,
    Nay, on me, too, thy hand I find.
Well I thy wisdom may adore,
    But never reach with earthy mind.

To shun thy notice, leave thine eye,
    O whither might I take my way?
        To starry sphere?
        Thy throne is there.
    To dead men's undelightsome stay?
There is thy walk, and there to lie
    Unknown in vain I should assay.

Giulio Casserius. *The Human Fetus.*
c. 1601. Copperplate from Adrian
Spigelius's book *De Formato Foetu.*

O sun, whom light nor flight can match,
  Suppose thy lightful, flightful wings
   Thou lend to me,
   And I could flee
  As far as thee the evening brings,
Even led to west he would me catch
  Nor should I lurk with western things.

Do thou thy best, O secret night,
  In sable veil to cover me,
   Thy sable veil
   Shall vainly fail;
  With day unmasked my night shall be,
For night is day, and darkness light,
  O father of all lights, to thee.

Each inmost piece in me is thine:
  While yet I in my mother dwelt,
   All that me clad
   From thee I had.
  Thou in my frame hast strangely dealt;
Needs in my praise thy works must shine,
  So inly them my thoughts have felt.

Thou, how my back was beam-wise laid
  And raftering of my ribs, dost know;
   Knowst every point
   Of bone and joint,
  How to this whole these parts did grow,
In brave embroidery fair arrayed
  Though wrought in shop both dark and low.

Nay, fashionless, ere form I took,
  Thy all-and-more-beholding eye
   My shapeless shape
   Could not escape;

All these, time-framed successively
Ere one had being, in the book
    Of thy foresight enrolled did lie.

My God, how I these studies prize
    That do thy hidden workings show!
        Whose sum is such
        No sum so much,
    Nay, summed as sand, they sumless grow.
I lie to sleep, from sleep I rise,
    Yet still in thought with thee I go.

My God, if thou but one wouldst kill,
    Then straight would leave my further chase
        This cursed brood
        Inured to blood
    Whose graceless taunts at thy disgrace
Have aimed oft, and, hating still,
    Would with proud lies thy truth outface.

Hate not I them, who thee do hate?
    Thine, Lord, I will the censure be.
        Detest I not
        The cankered knot
    Whom I against thee banded see?
O Lord, thou knowst in highest rate
    I hate them all as foes to me.

Search me, my God, and prove my heart,
    Examine me, and try my thought:
        And mark in me
        If aught there be
    That hath with cause their anger wrought.
If not (as not) my life's each part,
    Lord, safely guide from danger brought.

(see *Psalm 139*)

William Hogarth. *A Harlot's Progress*
(*Death,* Plate 5). c. 1730. Engraving,
approximately 18×25″. Courtesy of The
British Museum, London

39.

PROVIDE, PROVIDE

Robert Frost

The witch that came (the withered hag)
To wash the steps with pail and rag
Was once the beauty Abishag,

The picture pride of Hollywood.
Too many fall from great and good
For you to doubt the likelihood.

Die early and avoid the fate.
Or if predestined to die late,
Make up your mind to die in state.

Make the whole stock exchange your own!
If need be, occupy a throne,
Where nobody can call *you* crone.

Some have relied on what they knew,
Others on simply being true.
What worked for them might work for you.

No memory of having starred
Atones for later disregard
Or keeps the end from being hard.

Better to go down dignified
With boughten friendship at your side
Than none at all. Provide, provide!

(see *1 Kings 1:1–4*)

40.

SOLOMON TO SHEBA
William Butler Yeats

Sang Solomon to Sheba,
And kissed her dusky face,
"All day long from mid-day
We have talked in the one place,
All day long from shadowless noon
We have gone round and round
In the narrow theme of love
Like an old horse in a pound."

To Solomon sang Sheba,
Planted on his knees,
"If you had broached a matter
That might the learned please,
You had before the sun had thrown
Our shadows on the ground
Discovered that my thoughts, not it,
Are but a narrow pound."

Anonymous from Addis-Ababa.
*Ethiopian Storyboard of the Queen of Sheba
and King Solomon* (detail). n.d.
90½×34⅛″. Collection Musée de
l'Homme, Paris

Sang Solomon to Sheba,
And kissed her Arab eyes,
"There's not a man or woman
Born under the skies
Dare match in learning with us two,
And all day long we have found
There's not a thing but love can make
The world a narrow pound."

(see *1 Kings 10:1–13*)

41.

SONNET
Gerard Manley Hopkins

The shepherd's brow, fronting forked lightning, owns
The horror and the havoc and the glory
Of it. Angels fall, they are towers, from heaven—a story
Of just, majestical, and giant groans.
But man—we, scaffold of score brittle bones;
Who breathe, from groundlong babyhood to hoary
Age gasp; whose breath is our *memento mori*—
What bass is *our* viol for tragic tones?
He! Hand to mouth he lives, and voids with shame;
And, blazoned in however bold the name,
Man Jack the man is, just; his mate a hussy.
And I that die these deaths, that feed this flame,
That . . . in smooth spoons spy life's masque mirrored: tame
My tempests there, my fire and fever fussy.

(see *Isaiah 14*)

Paul Klee. *Angel Applicant.* 1939.
Gouache, black ink, and pencil on wove
paper, mounted on light cardboard,
19 ¼ × 13 ⅜″. The Metropolitan Museum
of Art, New York. The Berggruen Klee
Collection, 1984

O TO BE A DRAGON

Marianne Moore

If I, like Solomon, . . .
could have my wish—

my wish . . . O to be a dragon,
a symbol of the power of Heaven—of silkworm
size or immense; at times invisible.
Felicitous phenomenon!

(see *1 Kings 3:5–15*)

Unknown. *Dragon Robe. c.*
1675. Qing Dynasty,
China. Embroidery on silk,
length: 53″. Courtesy of the
Textile Department, Royal
Ontario Museum, Toronto

THE CITY IN THE SEA

Edgar Allan Poe

Lo! Death has reared himself a throne
In a strange city lying alone
Far down within the dim West,
Where the good and the bad and the worst and the best
Have gone to their eternal rest.
There shrines and palaces and towers
(Time-eaten towers that tremble not!)
Resemble nothing that is ours.
Around, by lifting winds forgot,
Resignedly beneath the sky
The melancholy waters lie.

No rays from the holy heaven come down
On the long night-time of that town;
But light from out the lurid sea
Streams up the turrets silently—
Gleams up the pinnacles far and free—
Up domes—up spires—up kingly halls—
Up fanes—up Babylon-like walls—
Up shadowy long-forgotten bowers
Of sculptured ivy and stone flowers—
Up many and many a marvelous shrine
Whose wreathéd friezes intertwine
The viol, the violet, and the vine.

Resignedly beneath the sky
The melancholy waters lie.
So blend the turrets and shadows there
That all seem pendulous in air
While from a proud tower in the town
Death looks gigantically down.

There open fanes and gaping graves
Yawn level with the luminous waves;
But not the riches there that lie
In each idol's diamond eye—
Not the gaily jeweled dead
Tempt the waters from their bed;
For no ripples curl, alas!
Along that wilderness of glass—
No swellings tell that winds may be
Upon some far-off happier sea—
No heavings hint that winds have been
On seas less hideously serene.

But lo, a stir is in the air!
The wave—there is a movement there!
As if the towers had thrust aside,
In slightly sinking, the dull tide—
As if their tops had feebly given
A void within the filmy Heaven.
The waves have now a redder glow—
The hours are breathing faint and low—
And when, amid no earthly moans,
Down, down that town shall settle hence,
Hell, rising from a thousand thrones,
Shall do it reverence.

(see *Isaiah 23:6–13; Ezekiel 26:15–27:36*)

Christian Schuessele and James M. Sommerville. *Ocean Life.* 1899. Watercolor, gum arabic, gouache, and graphite underdrawing on light green wove paper, 18⅞×27½". The Metropolitan Museum of Art, New York. Gift of Mr. and Mrs. Erving Wolf, 1977

Unknown. *Vision of Isaiah* from
Commentary. Late 10th–early 11th
century. Illuminated manuscript.
Staatsbibliothek, Bamberg, Germany

44.
MEDITATION TWELVE

Edward Taylor

Who is this that cometh from Edom, with dyed garments from
Bozrah? this that is glorious in his apparel, travelling in the greatness
of his strength? I that speak in righteousness, mighty to save.

This quest rapped at my ears broad golden doors:
      Who's this that comes from Edom in this shine,
In dyed robes from Bozrah? this more o'er
      All glorious in's apparel: all divine?
      Then through that wicket rushed this gust there gave:
      It's I that right do speak, mighty to save.

I threw through Zion's lattice then an eye
      Which spied one like a lump of glory pure:
Nay, clothes of gold buttoned with pearls do lie
      Like rags, or shoeclouts unto his he wore.
      Heaven's curtains blanched with sun, and stars of light
      Are black as sackcloth to his garments bright.

One shining sun gilding the skies with light,
      Benights all candles with their flaming blaze:
So doth the glory of this robe benight
      Ten thousand suns at once ten thousand ways.
      For every third therein's dyed with the shine
      Of all, and each the attributes divine.

The sweetest breath, the sweetest violet,
      Rose, or carnation ever did gust out,
Is but a foist to that perfume beset
      In thy apparel steaming round about.
      But is this so? My puling soul then pine
      In love until this lovely one be thine.

Pluck back the curtains, back the window shuts:
        Through Zion's agate window take a view,
How Christ in pinked robes from Bozrah puts,
        Comes glorious in's apparel forth to woo.
        Oh! if his glory ever kiss thine eye,
        Thy love will soon enchanted be thereby.

Then grieve, my soul, thy vessel is so small,
        And holds no more for such a lovely He.
That strength's so little, love scarce acts at all;
        That sight's so dim, doth scarce him lovely see.
        Grieve, grieve, my soul, thou shouldst so pimp
        Now such a price is here presented thee.

All sight's too little sight enough to make,
        All strength's too little love enough to rear,
All vessels are too small to hold or take
        Enough love up for such a lovely dear.
        How little to this little's then thy all,
        For him whose beauty saith all love's too small?

My lovely one, I fain would love thee much,
        But all my love is none at all I see;
Oh! let thy beauty give a glorious touch
        Upon my heart, and melt to love all me.
        Lord, melt me all up into love for thee,
        Whose loveliness excels what love can be.

(see Isaiah 63:1)

45.
BABYLON
Alfred Lord Tennyson

Bow, daughter of Babylon, bow thee to dust!
Thine heart shall be quelled, and thy pride shall be crushed:
Weep, Babylon, weep! for thy splendour is past;
And they come like the storm in the day of the blast.

Howl, desolate Babylon, lost one and lone!
And bind thee in sackcloth—for where is thy throne?
Like a winepress in wrath will I trample thee down,
And rend from thy temples the pride of thy crown.

Though thy streets be a hundred, thy gates be all brass,
Yet thy proud ones of war shall be withered like grass;
Thy gates shall be broken, thy strength be laid low,
And thy streets shall resound to the shouts of the foe!

Though thy chariots of power on thy battlements bound,
And the grandeur of waters encompass thee round;
Yet thy walls shall be shaken, thy waters shall fail,
Thy matrons shall shriek, and thy king shall be pale.

The terrible day of thy fall is at hand,
When my rage shall descend on the face of thy land;
The lances are pointed, the keen sword is bared,
The shields are anointed, the helmets prepared.

I call upon Cyrus! He comes from afar,
And the armies of nations are gathered to war;
With the blood of thy children his path shall be red,
And the bright sun of conquest shall blaze o'er his head.

Thou glory of kingdoms! thy princes are drunk,
But their loins shall be loosed, and their hearts shall be sunk;
They shall crouch to the dust, and be counted as slaves,
At the roll of his wheels, like the rushing of waves!

For I am the Lord, who have mightily spanned
The breadth of the heavens, and the sea and the land;
And the mountains shall flow at my presence, and earth
Shall reel to and fro in the glance of my wrath!

Your proud domes of cedar on earth shall be thrown
And the rank grass shall wave o'er the lonely hearthstone;
And your sons and your sires and your daughters shall bleed
By the barbarous hands of the murdering Mede!

I will sweep ye away in destruction and death,
As the whirlwind that scatters the chaff with its breath;
And the fanes of your gods shall be sprinkled with gore,
And the course of your streams shall be heard of no more!

There the wandering Arab shall ne'er pitch his tent,
But the beasts of the desert shall wail and lament;
In their desolate houses the dragons shall lie,
And the satyrs shall dance, and the bitterns shall cry!

(see Isaiah 13)

John Martin. *The Fall of Babylon.* 1831.
Mezzotint, 28½×18½″. Copyright The
British Museum, London

46.

ON FALLING ASLEEP BY FIRELIGHT

William Meredith

*The wolf and the lamb shall feed together, and the lion shall eat
straw like the bullock: and dust shall be the serpent's meat.*

Horace Pippin. *Holy Mountain II.* 1944.
Oil on fabric, 23×30″. Private collection

Around the fireplace, pointing at the fire,
As in the prophet's dream of the last truce,
The animals lie down; they doze or stare,
Their hoofs and paws in comical disuse;
A few still run in dreams. None seems aware
Of the laws of prey that lie asleep here, too,
The dreamer unafraid who keeps the zoo.

Some winter nights impel us to take in
Whatever lopes outside, beastly or kind;
Nothing that gibbers in or out of mind
But the hearth bestows a sleepy sense of kin.
Promiscuous hosts, we bid the causeless slime
Come in; its casualness remains a crime,
But metaphysics bites less sharp than wind.

Now, too, a ghostly, gradually erect
Company lies down, weary of the walk—
Parents with whom we would, but cannot, talk,
Beside them on the floor their artifacts:
Weapons we gave them, which they now bring back.
If they see our privilege, they do not object,
And we are not ashamed to be their stock.

All we had thought unkind were all the while
Alike, the firelight says, and strikes us dumb;
We dream there is no ravening or guile
And take it kindly of the beasts to come
And suffer hospitality, the heat
Turns softly on the hearth into that dust
Isaiah said would be the serpent's meat.

(see *Isaiah* 65:17–25)

109

47.

AHOLIBAH

Algernon Charles Swinburne

In the beginning God made thee
    A woman well to look upon,
Thy tender body as a tree
    Whereon cool wind hath always blown
    Till the clean branches be well grown.

There was none like thee in the land;
    The girls that were thy bondwomen
Did bind thee with a purple band
    Upon thy forehead, that all men
    Should know thee for God's handmaiden.

Strange raiment clad thee like a bride,
    With silk to wear on hands and feet
And plates of gold on either side:
    Wine made thee glad, and thou didst eat
    Honey, and choice of pleasant meat.

And fishers in the middle sea
    Did get thee sea-fish and sea-weeds
In colour like the robes on thee;
    And curious work of plaited reeds,
    And wools wherein live purple bleeds.

And round the edges of thy cup
    Men wrought thee marvels out of gold,
Strong snakes with lean throats lifted up,
    Large eyes whereon the brows had hold,
    And scaly things their slime kept cold.

For thee they blew soft wind in flutes
  And ground sweet roots for cunning scent;
Made slow because of many lutes,
  The wind among thy chambers went
  Wherein no light was violent.

God called thy name Aholibah,
  His tabernacle being in thee,
A witness through waste Asia;
  Thou wert a tent sewn cunningly
  With gold and colours of the sea.

God gave thee gracious ministers
  And all their work who plait and weave:
The cunning of embroiderers
  That sew the pillow to the sleeve,
  And likeness of all things that live.

Thy garments upon thee were fair
  With scarlet and with yellow thread;
Also the weaving of thine hair
  Was as fine gold upon thy head,
  And thy silk shoes were sewn with red.

All sweet things he bade sift, and ground
  As a man grindeth wheat in mills
With strong wheels alway going round;
  He gave thee corn, and grass that fills
  The cattle on a thousand hills.

The wine of many seasons fed
  Thy mouth, and made it fair and clean;
Sweet oil was poured out on thy head
  And ran down like cool rain between
  The strait close locks it melted in.

The strong men and the captains knew
        Thy chambers wrought and fashioned
With gold and covering of blue,
        And the blue raiment of thine head
        Who satest on a stately bed.

All these had on their garments wrought
        The shape of beasts and creeping things
The body that availeth not,
        Flat backs of worms and veinèd wings,
        And the lewd bulk that sleeps and stings.

Also the chosen of the years,
        The multitude being at ease,
With sackbuts and with dulcimers
        And noise of shawms and psalteries
        Made mirth within the ears of these.

But as a common woman doth,
        Thou didst think evil and devise;
The sweet smell of thy breast and mouth
        Thou madest as the harlot's wise,
        And there was painting on thine eyes.

Yea, in the woven guest-chamber
        And by the painted passages
Where the strange gracious paintings were,
        State upon state of companies,
        There came on thee the lust of these.

Because of shapes on either wall
        Sea-coloured from some rare blue shell
At many a Tyrian interval,
        Horsemen on horses, girdled well,
        Delicate and desirable,

Sir Edward Burne-Jones. *The Sleeping Beauty* from The Briar Rose Series. 1871. Oil on canvas, 24×46″. Museo de Arte de Ponce, Puerto Rico. Luis A. Ferré Foundation, Inc.

Thou saidest: I am sick of love:
  Stay me with flagons, comfort me
With apples for my pain thereof
  Till my hands gather in his tree
  That fruit wherein my lips would be.

Yea, saidest thou, I will go up
  When there is no more shade than one
May cover with a hollow cup,
  And make my bed against the sun
  Till my blood's violence be done.

Thy mouth was leant upon the wall
      Against the painted mouth, thy chin
Touched the hair's painted curve and fall;
      Thy deep throat, fallen lax and thin,
      Worked as the blood's beat worked therein.

Therefore, O thou Aholibah,
      God is not glad because of thee;
And thy fine gold shall pass away
      Like those fair coins of ore that be
      Washed over by the middle sea.

Then will one make thy body bare
      To strip it of all gracious things,
And pluck the cover from thine hair,
      And break the gift of many kings,
      Thy wrist-rings and thine ankle-rings.

Likewise the man whose body joins
      To thy smooth body, as was said,
Who hath a girdle on his loins
      And dyed attire upon his head—
      The same who, seeing, worshipped,

Because thy face was like the face
      Of a clean maiden that smells sweet,
Because thy gait was as the pace
      Of one that opens not her feet
      And is not heard within the street—

Even he, O thou Aholibah,
      Made separate from thy desire,
Shall cut thy nose and ears away
      And bruise thee for thy body's hire
      And burn the residue with fire.

Then shall the heathen people say,
		The multitude being at ease;
Lo, this is that Aholibah
		Whose name was blown among strange seas,
		Grown old with soft adulteries.

Also her bed was made of green,
		Her windows beautiful for glass
That she had made her bed between:
		Yea, for pure lust her body was
		Made like white summer-coloured grass.

Her raiment was a strongman's spoil;
		Upon a table by a bed
She set mine incense and mine oil
		To be the beauty of her head
		In chambers walled about with red.

Also between the walls she had
		Fair faces of strong men portrayed;
All girded round the loins, and clad
		With several cloths of woven braid
		And garments marvelously made.

Therefore the wrath of God shall be
		Set as a watch upon her way;
And whoso findeth by the sea
		Blown dust of bones will hardly say
		If this were that Aholibah.

(see Ezekiel 23)

Peter Paul Rubens. Copy after
Michelangelo's *Daniel*. Crayon,
17¾ × 13⅝″. Musée du Louvre, Paris

48.

NEBUCHADNEZZAR
Elinor Wylie

My body is weary to death of my mischievous brain;
I am weary forever and ever of being brave;
Therefore I crouch on my knees while the cool white rain
Curves the clover over my head like a wave.

The stem and the frosty seed of the grass are ripe;
I have devoured their strength; I have drunk them deep;
And the dandelion is gall in a thin green pipe;
But the clover is honey and sun and the smell of sleep.

(see *Daniel 2*)

49.

NEBUCHADNEZZAR'S DREAM
John Keats

Before he went to feed with owls and bats
    Nebuchadnezzar had an ugly dream,
    Worse than an Hus'if's when she thinks her cream
Made a Naumachia for mice and rats.
        So scared, he sent for that "Good King of Cats"
Young Daniel, who soon did pluck the beam
    From out his eye, and said "I do not deem
        Your sceptre worth a straw—your Cushions old door-mats."
A horrid nightmare similar somewhat
    Of late has haunted a most valiant crew
        Of loggerheads and Chapmen—we are told
That any Daniel though he be a sot
    Can make their lying lips turn pale of hue
        By drawling out "ye are that head of Gold."

(see *Daniel 3*)

THE SPERMACETI WHALE
Beale

Stewart del^t

Attributed to Louis Thiercelin. *The
Spermaceti Whale.* c. 1837. Engraving,
4×6½″. Mansell Collection, London

PLATE 10.

50.

THE RIBS AND TERRORS

Herman Melville

The ribs and terrors in the whale,
      Arched over me a dismal gloom,
While all God's sun-lit waves rolled by,
      And lift me to a deeper doom.

I saw the opening maw of hell,
      With endless pains and sorrows there;
Which none but they that feel can tell—
      Oh, I was plunging to despair.

In black distress, I called my God,
      When I could scarce believe him mine,
He bowed his ear to my complaints—
      No more the whale did me confine.

With speed he flew to my relief,
      As on a radiant dolphin borne;
Awful, yet bright, as lightning shone
      The face of my Deliverer God.

My song for ever shall record
      That terrible, that joyful hour;
I give the glory to my God,
      His all the mercy and the power.

(see *Jonah 2*)

51

FROM LIFE TO LOVE
Countee Cullen

Four winds and seven seas have called me friend,
And countless roads have known my restless feet;
Deep crystal springs and pollened buds were sweet
For sustenance their princely fare to lend,
While nameless birds from grove and blossomed bend
Deluged my soul with song; if it were meet
To love Life so, then Love will but complete
My joy, for Life with Love can never end.
Love, I have heard the sweet of your voice, have seen
You pass the dawn-flushed singing hills between;
Now suppliant I kneel and pray you show
The mercied sceptre favored Esther saw;
The dawn in me has broke, and well I know
That Love is king and creed and Persian law.

(see Esther 7)

Filippino Lippi. *Esther at the Palace Gate.*
1475–80. Tempera on poplar,
19×17×1¼″. National Gallery of
Canada, Ottawa

Kenneth Snelson. *Brooklyn Bridge.*
1980. Photograph

52.

TO BROOKLYN BRIDGE
Hart Crane

From going to and fro in the earth,
and from walking up and down in it.

How many dawns, chill from his rippling rest
The seagull's wings shall dip and pivot him,
Shedding white rings of tumult, building high
Over the chained bay waters Liberty—

Then with inviolate curve, forsake our eyes
As apparitional as sails that cross
Some page of figures to be filed away;
—Till elevators drop us from our day . . .

I think of cinemas, panoramic sleights
With multitudes bent toward some flashing scene
Never disclosed, but hastened to again,
Foretold to other eyes on the same screen;

And Thee, across the harbor, silver-paced
As though the sun took step of thee, yet left
Some motion ever unspent in thy stride,—
Implicitly thy freedom staying thee!

Out of some subway scuttle, cell or loft
A bedlamite speeds to thy parapets,
Tilting there momently, shrill shirt ballooning,
A jest falls from the speechless caravan.

Down Wall, from girder into street noon leaks,
A rip-tooth of the sky's acetylene;
All afternoon the cloud-flown derricks turn . . .
Thy cables breathe the North Atlantic still.

And obscure as that heaven of the Jews,
Thy guerdon . . . Accolade thou dost bestow
Of anonymity time cannot raise:
Vibrant reprieve and pardon thou dost show.

O harp and altar, of the fury fused,
(How could mere toil align thy choiring strings!)
Terrific threshold of the prophet's pledge,
Prayer of pariah, and the lover's cry,—

Again the traffic lights that skim thy swift
Unfractioned idiom, immaculate sigh of stars,
Beading thy path—condense eternity:
And we have seen night lifted in thine arms.

Under thy shadow by the piers I waited;
Only in darkness is thy shadow clear.
The City's fiery parcels all undone,
Already snow submerges an iron year . . .

O Sleepless as the river under thee,
Vaulting the sea, the prairies' dreaming sod,
Unto us lowliest sometime sweep, descend
And of the curveship lend a myth to God.

(see Job 1:7)

123

53.

Cæsura

John Ashbery

Job sat in a corner of the dump eating asparagus
With one hand and scratching his unsightly eruptions
With the other. Pshaw, it'd blow over. In the office
They'd like discussing it. His thoughts

Were with the office now: how protected it was,
Though still a place to work. Sit up straight, the
Monitor inside said. It worked for a second
But didn't improve the posture of his days, taken

As a cross section of the times. Correction: of our time.
And it was (it was again): "Have you made your list up?
I have one ambulance three nuns two (black-
And-white list) cops dressed as Keystone Kops lists, a red light

At leafy intersection list." Then it goes blank, pulp-color.
Until at the end where they give out the list
Of awardees. The darkness and light have returned. It was still
The weather of the soul, vandalized, out-at-elbow. A blight. Spared, though.

(see *Job* 2:8)

Jean Colombe. *Job on His Dung Heap.*
From *Les Très Riches Heures du Duc de
Berry* (Ms. 65/1284, f. 82r). c. 1485.
Illuminated manuscript. Musée Condé,
Chantilly, France

PLACEBO DILEXI QVONIAM EXAVDIET DNS VOCE ORA

54.

LEVIATHAN

from *Job Triumphant*

Joshua Sylvester

Canst thou hale up the huge leviathan,
With hook and line amid the ocean?
Canst thou his tongue with steely crotchets thrill;
Or with a thorn his snuffing nose, or gill?
Will he come sue, by supplications, to thee?
Will he, with smooth and soothing speeches, woo thee?
Will he by covenant serve thee, at thy beck;
Or be thy slave, for ever at thy check?
Wilt thou with him, as with a sparrow, play?
And give him, tied, unto thy girls, away?
Shall fishermen of him a feast prepare?
Shall they his flesh among the merchants share?
Canst thou his skin with barbed pheons pierce?
Or plant his head with groves of otter spears?
        Lay hold on him: set on him: but, before
Think on the battle, and come there no more.
For 'tis so far from hope of victory,
That even his sight would rather make thee fly.
There's none so fierce that dares him rouse or hunt.
        Then, who shall safely me my self affront?
Who hath prevented me? To whom have I
Been first beholding for a courtesy,
Or bound at all for any benefit
Bestowed on me, that I should guerdon it?
Why? is not all earth's ample arms confine,
All under heaven, all in the ocean, mine?
        I will not hide his parts and properties;
Neither his strength, nor seemly symmetries.
Who shall unhood him? Who with double rein
Shall bridle him, with snaffle, trench, or chain?

Or put the bit between his jaws (his portal)
Impaled with terror of his teeth so mortal?
His shield-like scales, he chiefly glories in,
So close compact, glued, sealed; that, between,
No air can enter, nor no engine pierce,
Nor any point disjoin them or disperse.

     His neesings cause a light, as brightly burning;
His eyes are like the eyelids of the morning;
Out of his mouth flow blazing lamps, and fly
Quick sparks of fire, ascending swift and high:
Out of his nostrils, smoke, as from a pot,
Kettle or caldron when it boileth hot:
His breath doth kindle coals, when with the same
He whirleth out a storm of fume and flame:
Strength dwelleth in his neck; so that he joys
In saddest storms, and triumphs of annoys:
His flakes of flesh as solid to his bone;
His heart's as hard as windmill's nether-stone.

     To see him rise, and how he breaks withal;
The stoutest stoop, and to their prayers fall.
No weapons of defence, or of offence,
Can him offend, or from him be defence:
Iron and brass he weighs as sticks and straw:
Slingstones and arrows, him do never awe:
Darts daunt him not, more than they stubble were:
He laugheth at the shaking of a spear:
Sharp ragged stones, keen pointed shards and shells,
He resteth on, amid his muddy cells.
He makes the deep sea like a pot to boil,
A pot of ointment (casting scummy soil):

Julien Menu. *Imaginary Whale.* n.d. Oil
on canvas. Private collection

Where he hath past, he leaves upon the streams
A shining path, and the ocean hoary seems.

      In earth is nothing like him to be seen;
So fearless made, so full of haughty spleen;
Despising all high things, himself beside.
He is the King of all the Sons of Pride.

(see Job 41)

55.

THE MORNING STARS

Robert Lax

Have you seen my circus?

Have you known such a thing?

Did you get up in the early morning and see the wagons pull into town?

Did you see them occupy the field?

Were you there when it was set up?

Did you see the cook-house set up in dark by lantern-light?

Did you see them build the fire and sit around it smoking and talking quietly?

As the first rays of dawn came, did you see

Them roll in blankets and go to sleep?

A little sleep until time came to

Unroll the canvas, raise the tent,

Draw and carry water for the men and animals;

Were you there when the animals came forth,

The great lumbering elephants to drag the poles

And unroll the canvas?

Were you there when the morning moved over the grasses?

Were you there when the sun looked through dark bars of clouds

At the men who slept by the cook-house fire?

Did you see the morning star twinkle in the firmament?

Have you heard the voices of the men's slow muttering,

Have you heard their laughter around the cook-house fire?

When the morning stars threw down their spears, and watered heaven . . .

Have you looked at spheres of dew on spears of grass?

Have you watched the light of a star through a world of dew?

Have you seen the morning move over the grasses?

And to each leaf the morning is present.

Were you there when we stretched out the line,

Mark Rothko. *Number 101*. 1961. Oil
on canvas, 79×81″. Private collection

When we rolled out the sky,
When we set up the firmament?
Were you there when the morning stars
Sang together
And all the sons of God shouted for joy?

(see *Job 38–39*)

Joseph Cornell. *The Journeying Sun for Samuel Taylor Coleridge.* 1963. Collage and ink, 9¼×8¾". Collection Dore Ashton

56.

THE LORD, THE LORD MY SHEPHERD

Sir Philip Sidney

The Lord, the Lord my shepherd is,
    And so can never I
       Taste misery.
He rests me in green pasture his:
    By waters still, and sweet
       He guides my feet.

He me revives: leads me the way,
    Which righteousness doth take,
       For his name's sake.
Yea though I should through valleys stray,
    Of death's dark shade, I will
       No whit fear ill.

For thou, dear Lord, thou me besett'st:
    Thy rod, and thy staff be
       To comfort me;
Before me thou a table sett'st,
    Even when foes envious eye
       Doth it espy.

Thou oil'st my head, thou fill'st my cup:
    Nay more thou endless good,
       Shalt give me food.
To thee, I say, ascended up,
    Where thou, the Lord of all,
       Dost hold thy hall.

(see Psalm 23)

57

THE DEAD WILL NOT PRAISE YOU

David Shapiro

for Cantor Berele Chagy

My grandfather emerges
in a synagogue
with familiar accents
unlike his noble voice
a pudgy little man
sweet tenor *coloratura flautando*
He marches down the aisle
with a blue white crown
Women ask questions
and they are charmed
and he is beloved
like etymology
Is my mother in attendance
or is she dead?
What are questions now?
Are the dead permitted: to
sing? Is he serious?
Are the dead permitted
to return and sing?

(see *Psalm 88*)

Arnold Schwartzman. 1990. *Gravestone,*
Karczew, Poland. Photograph

Hans Mielich. *Chamber Music* in *Neue
Veste* in Munich Codex, Pentitential
Psalms. 1565–70. Parchment, 23 × 16¾".
Bayerische Staatsbibliothek, Munich

58.

TO HIM WITH TRUMPETS

Sir John Davies

To him with trumpets and with flutes,
With cornets, clarions, and with lutes,
With harps, with organs, and with shawms,
With holy anthems and with psalms,
With voice of angels and of men,
Sing Aleluyia: amen, amen.

(see *Psalm 150*)

59.

PARAPHRASE

Samuel Johnson

Turn on the prudent ant thy heedless eyes,
Observe her labours, sluggard, and be wise;
No stern command, no monitory voice,
Prescribes her duties, or directs her choice;
Yet, timely provident, she hastes away
To snatch the blessings of a plenteous day;
When fruitful summer loads the teeming plain,
She crops the harvest and she stores the grain.
How long shall sloth usurp thy useless hours,
Unnerve thy vigour, and enchain thy powers?
While artful shades thy downy couch enclose,
And soft solicitation courts repose,
Amidst the drowsy charms of dull delight,
Year chases year with unremitted flight,
Till want now following, fraudulent and slow,
Shall spring to seize thee, like an ambushed foe.

(see *Proverbs 6:6–11*)

M. C. Escher. *Moebius Strip II (Red Ants)*.
1963. Woodcut in red, black and gray-
green, 17⅞×8⅛″. M. C. Escher
Foundation. Baarn, Holland

Hieronymus Bosch (1453–1516). *The
Hay Wain* (center panel of triptych). Oil
on panel, 53⅛×39⅜". The Prado, Madrid

60.

CHARMS AND KNOTS

George Herbert

Who read a chapter when they rise,
Shall ne'er be troubled with ill eyes.

A poor man's rod, when thou dost ride,
Is both a weapon and a guide.

Who shuts his hand, hath lost his gold:
Who opens it, hath it twice told.

Who goes to bed and doth not pray,
Maketh two nights to every day.

Who by aspersions throw a stone
At the head of others, hit their own.

Who looks on ground with humble eyes,
Finds himself there, and seeks to rise.

When the hair is sweet through pride or lust,
The powder doth forget the dust.

Take one from ten, and what remains?
Ten still, if sermons go for gains.

In shallow waters heaven doth show;
But who drinks on, to hell may go.

(see Proverbs)

61

'A SERVANT WHEN HE REIGNETH'

Rudyard Kipling

For three things the earth is diquieted, and for four
which it cannot bear: For a servant when he reigneth; and
a fool when he is filled with meat; For an odious woman when
she is married; and a handmaid that is heir to her mistress.

Three things make earth unquiet
And four she cannot brook
The godly Agur counted them
And put them in a book—
Those Four Tremendous Curses
With which mankind is cursed;
But a Servant when He Reigneth
Old Agur entered first.

An Handmaid that is Mistress
We need not call upon.
A Fool when he is full of Meat
Will fall asleep anon.
An Odious Woman Married
May bear a babe and mend;
But a Servant when He Reigneth
Is Confusion to the end.

His feet are swift to tumult,
His hands are slow to toil,
His ears are deaf to reason,
His lips are loud in broil.
He knows no use for power
Except to show his might.
He gives no heed to judgment
Unless it prove him right.

Because he served a master
Before his Kingship came,
And hid in all disaster
Behind his master's name,
So, when his Folly opens
The unnecessary hells,
A Servant when He Reigneth
Throws the blame on some one else.

His vows are lightly spoken,
His faith is hard to bind,
His trust is easy broken,
He fears his fellow-kind.
The nearest mob will move him
To break the pledge he gave—
Oh, a Servant when He Reigneth
Is more than ever slave!

(see *Proverbs* 30:21–23)

Max Ernst. *All Doors Look Alike* (Toutes
les portes se resemblent). 1929. From
La femme 100 têtes

Balthus. *The Turkish Room*. 1963–66.
Casein tempera with marble powder on
canvas, 70½×82½". Musée National
d'Art Moderne, Center Georges
Pompidou, Paris

62.

SANDALWOOD COMES TO MY MIND

Carl Rakosi

Sandalwood comes to my mind
when I think of you
and the triumph of your shoulders.
Greek chorus girls came to me
in the course of the day
and from a distance
Celtic vestals too,
but you bring me the Holy Land
and the sound of deep themes
in the inner chamber.

I give you praise
in the language
of wells and vineyards.

Your hand recalls
the salty heat of barbarism.
Your mouth is a pouch
for the accents of queens.
Your eyes flow over
with a gentle psalm
like the fawn eyes
of the woodland.
Your black hair
plucks my strings.

In the foggy wilderness
is not your heart
a hermit thrush?

You are timeless
as the mirrors,
Jewess of the palm country,
isolate as the frost
on the queen of swans.

Now that I have seen
the royal stones and fountains
and the tetrarch's lovely swans,
I am satisfied that you are
a mindful of white birds
in the folly of an old Jew.

Because of the coral
of your two breasts
are the prophets angry
but I have my lips upon them
and the song shall go on.

(see Song of Solomon 4:8–15)

63.

'ALL IS VANITY, SAITH THE PREACHER'
George Noel Gordon, Lord Byron

Fame, wisdom, love, and power were mine,
      And health and youth possessed me;
My goblets blushed from every vine,
      And lovely forms caressed me;
I sunned my heart in beauty's eyes,
      And felt my soul grow tender;
All earth can give, or mortal prize,
      Was mine of regal splendour.

I strive to number o'er what days
      Remembrance can discover,
Which all that life or earth displays
      Would lure me to live over.
There rose no day, there rolled no hour
      Of pleasure unembittered;
And not a trapping decked my power
      That galled not while it glittered.

The serpent of the field, by art
      And spells, is won from harming;
But that which coils around the heart,
      Oh! who hath power of charming?
It will not list to wisdom's lore,
      Nor music's voice can lure it;
But there it stings for evermore
      The soul that must endure it.

(see *Ecclesiastes 12:8*)

Muhammed Ali. *Poet in a Garden.* c.
1610. Gouache on paper, $4\frac{13}{16} \times 4\frac{1}{16}''$.
Museum of Fine Arts, Boston

64

THE CONCLUSION OF THE MATTER

Christopher Smart

Fear God—obey his just decrees,
And do it hand, and heart, and knees;
For after all our utmost care
There's nought like penitence and prayer.

Then weigh the balance in your mind,
Look forward, not one glance behind;
Let no foul fiend retard your pace,
Hosanna! Thou hast won the race.

(see Ecclesiastes 12:13)

William Blake. *Song of Los.* 1795.
Printed book, copy C, approximately
9×7″. The Pierpont Morgan Library,
New York. PML 77236

ACKNOWLEDGMENTS

THANKS TO MY wife Andrea and my daughter Aiah; to Robert Atwan and David Shapiro, who pointed me toward new poems for this book; to my editor at Abrams, Ellen Rosefsky; to Neil Hoos for help finding pictures and clearing permissions; to Darilyn Carnes for designing the book and cover; and last and first to Paul Gottlieb, who suggested I do the work, and found it good enough.

INDEX OF POETS

INDEX OF ARTISTS